CORNMEAL AND CIDER
Food and Drink in
the 1800s

DAILY LIFE IN AMERICA IN THE 1800s

N CREST PUBLISHERS INC.
eed Road
all, Pennsylvania 19008
MCP-BOOK (toll free)
.masoncrest.com

rinting
6 5 4 3 2 1

Library of Congress Cataloging-in-Publication Data

ain, Zachary.
meal and cider : food and drink in the 1800s / by Zachary Chastain.
. cm. — (Daily life in America in the 1800's)
ades bibliographical references and index.
  978-1-4222-1777-1 (hardcover)   ISBN (series) 978-1-4222-1774-0
  978-1-4222-1850-1 (pbk.)   ISBN (pbk series) 978-1-4222-1847-1
od habits—United States—History—19th century. 2. Drinking customs—United
s—History—19th century. 3. United States—History—19th century. 4. United
s—Social life and customs—19th century. I. Title.
853.U5C53 2011
.1'209034—dc22
                              2010015262

ced by Harding House Publishing Service, Inc.
v.hardinghousepages.com
ior Design by MK Bassett-Harvey.
r design by Torque Advertising + Design.
ed in USA by Bang Printing.

CORNMEAL AND CIDER
Food and Drink in
the 1800s

by
Zachary Chastain

Mason Crest Publishers

C
li
m
re

M
3
Br
(8
w

Fi
9

Ch
C

I
IS
IS
1.
St
St
G
3

Pr
wu
Int
Co
Pri

CORNMEAL AND CIDER
Food and Drink in the 1800s

by
Zachary Chastain

Mason Crest Publishers

MASON CREST PUBLISHERS INC.
370 Reed Road
Broomall, Pennsylvania 19008
(866)MCP-BOOK (toll free)
www.masoncrest.com

First Printing
9 8 7 6 5 4 3 2 1

Library of Congress Cataloging-in-Publication Data

Chastain, Zachary.
  Cornmeal and cider : food and drink in the 1800s / by Zachary Chastain.
     p. cm. — (Daily life in America in the 1800's)
  Includes bibliographical references and index.
  ISBN 978-1-4222-1777-1 (hardcover)   ISBN (series) 978-1-4222-1774-0
  ISBN 978-1-4222-1850-1 (pbk.)   ISBN (pbk series) 978-1-4222-1847-1
  1. Food habits—United States—History—19th century. 2. Drinking customs—United
States—History—19th century. 3. United States—History—19th century. 4. United
States—Social life and customs—19th century. I. Title.
  GT2853.U5C53 2011
  394.1'209034—dc22
                              2010015262

Produced by Harding House Publishing Service, Inc.
www.hardinghousepages.com
Interior Design by MK Bassett-Harvey.
Cover design by Torque Advertising + Design.
Printed in USA by Bang Printing.

Contents

Introduction

History can too often seem a parade of distant figures whose lives have no connection to our own. It need not be this way, for if we explore the history of the games people play, the food they eat, the ways they transport themselves, how they worship and go to war—activities common to all generations—we close the gap between past and present. Since the 1960s, historians have learned vast amounts about daily life in earlier periods. This superb series brings us the fruits of that research, thereby making meaningful the lives of those who have gone before.

The authors' vivid, fascinating descriptions invite young readers to journey into a past that is simultaneously strange and familiar. The 1800s were different, but, because they experienced the beginnings of the same baffling modernity were are still dealing with today, they are also similar. This was the moment when millennia of agrarian existence gave way to a new urban, industrial era. Many of the things we take for granted, such as speed of transportation and communication, bewildered those who were the first to behold the steam train and the telegraph. Young readers will be interested to learn that growing up then was no less confusing and difficult then than it is now, that people were no more in agreement on matters of religion, marriage, and family then than they are now.

We are still working through the problems of modernity, such as environmental degradation, that people in the nineteenth century experienced for the first time. Because they met the challenges with admirable ingenuity, we can learn much from them. They left behind a treasure trove of alternative living arrangements, cultures, entertainments, technologies, even diets that are even more relevant today. Students cannot help but be intrigued, not just by the technological ingenuity of those times, but by the courage of people who forged new frontiers, experimented with ideas and social arrangements. They will be surprised by the degree to which young people were engaged in the great events of the time, and how women joined men in the great adventures of the day.

When history is viewed, as it is here, from the bottom up, it becomes clear just how much modern America owes to the genius of ordinary people, to the labor of slaves and immigrants, to women as well as men, to both young people and adults. Focused on home and family life, books in this series provide insight into how much of history is made within the intimate spaces of private life rather than in the remote precincts of public power. The 1800s were the era of the self-made man and women, but also of the self-made communities. The past offers us a plethora of heroes and heroines together with examples of extraordinary collective action from the Underground Railway to the creation of the American trade union movement. There is scarcely an immigrant or ethic organization in America today that does not trace its origins to the nineteenth century.

This series is exceptionally well illustrated. Students will be fascinated by the images of both rural and urban life; and they will be able to find people their own age in these marvelous depictions of play as well as work. History is best when it engages our imagination, draws us out of our own time into another era, allowing us to return to the present with new perspectives on ourselves. My first engagement with the history of daily life came in sixth grade when my teacher, Mrs. Polster, had us do special projects on the history of the nearby Erie Canal. For the first time, history became real to me. It has remained my passion and my compass ever since.

The value of this series is that it opens up a dialogue with a past that is by no means dead and gone but lives on in every dimension of our daily lives. When history texts focus exclusively on political events, they invariably produce a sense of distance. This series creates the opposite effect by encouraging students to see themselves in the flow of history. In revealing the degree to which people in the past made their own history, students are encouraged to imagine themselves as being history-makers in their own right. The realization that history is not something apart from ourselves, a parade that passes us by, but rather an ongoing pageant in which we are all participants, is both exhilarating and liberating, one that connects our present not just with the past but also to a future we are responsible for shaping.

—*Dr. John Gillis, Rutgers University Professor of History Emeritus*

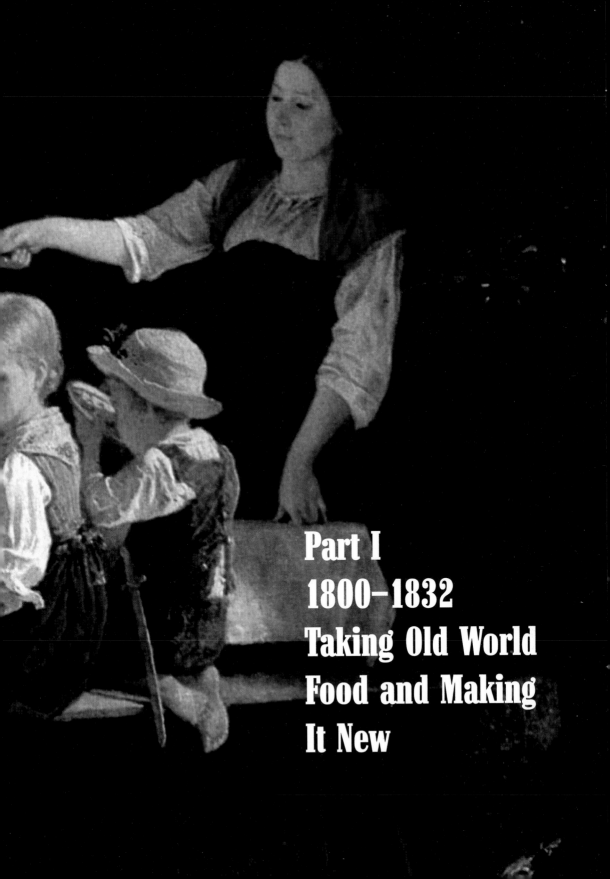

Part I
1800–1832
Taking Old World
Food and Making
It New

1800

1800 The Library of Congress is established.

1801

1801 The inventor of condensed milk, Gail Borden, is born. His company, New York Condensed Milk, revolutionizes how milk is processed.

1801 Thomas Jefferson is elected as the third President of the United States.

1803

1803 Louisiana Purchase—The United States purchases land from France and begins westward exploration.

1816

1816 Crop failures in Europe, food riots in England and France. Many Europeans begin to look to America for a better future.

1820

1820 Missouri Compromise— Agreement passes between pro-slavery and abolitionist groups. States that all the Louisiana Purchase territory north of the southern boundary of Missouri (except for Missouri) will be free states, and the territory south of that line will be slave.

1823

1823 Monroe Doctrine— States that any efforts made by Europe to colonize or interfere with land owned by the United States will be viewed as aggression and require military intervention.

1804

1804 Journey of Lewis and Clark— Lewis and Clark lead a team of explorers westward to the Columbia River in Oregon

1806

1806 Apple cider mill is patented by Isaac Quintard.

1812

1812 War of 1812— Fought between the United States and the United Kingdom

of the 1800s

1825

1825 The Erie Canal is completed— This allows direct transportation between the Great Lakes and the Atlantic Ocean.

1829

1829 The Yuengling Brewery opens in Pennsylvania. It will remain open permanently, becoming the oldest brewery in the United States.

1830

1830 The "Frugal Housewife" published by Lydia Maria Francis Child. Outlines hundreds of recipes for the common American household.

1830 (-39) US Agri- cultural exports $74 million a year during the 1830s- higher than any previous decade.

Bringing the Old Word to the New

In the year 1800, the United States was still an infant nation. It had only been independent for twenty-four years.

The Revolutionary War might have rid the new nation of British rule and declared the United States an independent nation, but it certainly did not cut all ties to England. For many U.S. citizens, England (and Europe) continued to be extremely important to their lives.

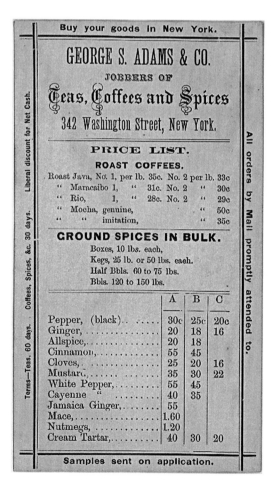

Buy your goods in New York.

GEORGE S. ADAMS & CO.

JOBBERS OF

Teas, Coffees and Spices

342 Washington Street, New York.

PRICE LIST.

ROAST COFFEES.

Roast Java, No. 1, per lb. 35c. No. 2 per lb. 33c
" Maracaibo 1, " 31c. No. 2 " 30c
" Rio, 1, " 28c. No. 2 " 29c
" Mocha, genuine, " 50c
" " imitation, " 35c

GROUND SPICES IN BULK.

Boxes, 10 lbs. each,
Kegs, 25 lb. or 50 lbs. each.
Half Bbls. 60 to 75 lbs.
Bbls. 120 to 150 lbs.

	A	B	C
Pepper, (black)	30c	25c	20c
Ginger,	20	18	16
Allspice,	20	18	
Cinnamon,	55	45	
Cloves,	25	20	16
Mustard,	35	30	22
White Pepper,	55	45	
Cayenne "	40	35	
Jamaica Ginger,	55		
Mace,	1.60		
Nutmegs,	1.20		
Cream Tartar,	40	30	20

Samples sent on application.

Liberal discount for Net Cash.

Coffees, Spices, &c. 30 days.

Terms—Teas, 60 days.

All orders by Mail promptly attended to.

Without England, the United States would scarcely have had an economy at all. Southerners sent huge crops of tobacco and cotton overseas, while citizens from the South and North relied on Europe (and England in particular) for manufactured goods and fancy foods of all sorts.

But it wasn't only economics that kept the "New World" tied to the "Old World." English culture dominated life in the United States right through the twentieth century—and food was a big part of that culture. Although each American region developed styles of cooking and eating unique to its place, each also kept its own English roots. New England, for instance, was founded on strict religious principles that considered spice and intense flavorings as sensual pleasures to be avoided. So they developed cooking traditions based on blander flavors, using boiling and baking, as well as incorporating new regional foods such as lobster. In the South, where overseas trade was common because of the plantation system, spices were more plentiful. There one was likely to find food influences from around the world, including Span-

Beginning in the 1700s, apple cider was America's most popular beverage. The early English colonists had brought apple seeds with them when they came to North America, and Johnny Appleseed spread apple trees to the Midwest as well. Made in presses like that shown here, cider (especially hard cider) was considered to be a healthy drink. Drinking cider was, in fact, usually healthier than drinking water in the 19th century, since water was often contaminated with bacteria.

ish, African, and Indian. Wherever you looked, you found Americans mixing the old with the new, and creating a whole new kind of regional cuisine.

Regions Are Important

Remember that in 1800 innovations in transportation such as the train and automobile had not been invented. The kinds of food people ate were largely determined by where they lived. This meant that the diet of an ordinary New Englander was quite different from the diet of an ordinary Southerner. Most Americans were settlers from Europe, and brought their European diets and styles of cooking along with them. But once separated from Europe by thousands of miles of ocean, they were forced to adopt styles of cooking and foods that were distinctly American, and distinctly regional. Only the wealthy could afford the expensive spices, teas, coffees, and baked goods that came from the Old World (Europe).

In the early 1800s, various "American" substitutes for European traditions were still being tested. Substituting corn-cake (also called "johnny cake") for wheat-based bread was a common example of this American substitution. Because it was difficult to grow wheat in the New England climate, settlers found that it wasn't reasonable to have wheat bread at every meal, so what once was a part of every day meals became a luxury for special occasions only.

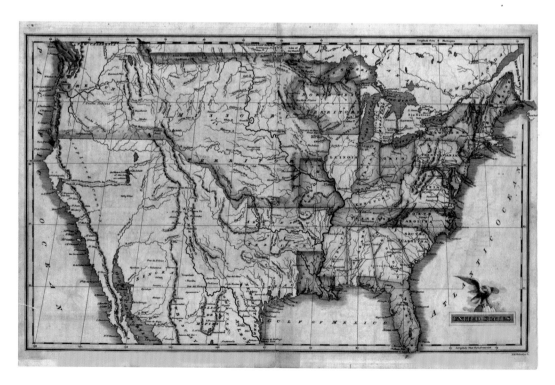

JOHNNY CAKE

1 cup stone ground corn meal (white or yellow)
1 cup boiling water
1 teaspoon salt
1 teaspoon sugar (optional)
milk
butter (or bacon drippings or oil or fat)

Stir together cornmeal, salt and sugar (if used). Bring water to a boil and pour over the meal mixture, stirring to prevent lumps. Let the batter rest 10 minutes.

Butter a large skillet or griddle and bring it to about 375 degrees, just to a sizzle (do not burn the butter). Add enough milk (1/2 to a cup) to the batter to make it the consistency of mashed potatoes, and drop by spoonfuls to make cakes about 2 or 3 inches wide and several inches apart (they will spread).

Let the cakes sizzle on the grill for about 6 to 11 minutes, until they are a deep golden brown on the bottom and slightly firm on the top, before turning them over.

Add some more butter to the griddle—or place a thin pat of butter on each cake, before turning them over and cooking for another 6 minutes (or longer), until they are a deep golden brown color.

Makes about 8 cakes. Serve with butter and maple syrup.

New Englanders were forced to try new ways of finding nourishment and preserving food through the cold winter months. One way in which New Englanders adapted to their new climate was to add more seafood to their diet. Like all Americans of that time, they needed to adapt to their new climate and geography in order to survive. Out of necessity, the Atlantic Ocean became a major source for their food.

If you lived near the ocean, seafood was plentiful.

CHOWDER

Mary Randolph, cousin of Mary Custis (the wife of General Robert E. Lee) and a first cousin of Thomas Jefferson, included this recipe in her book "The Virginia Housewife," published in 1828:

Take any kind of firm fish, cut it in pieces six inches long, sprinkle salt and pepper over each piece, cover the bottom of a small Dutch oven with slices of salt pork about half boiled, lay in the fish, strewing a little chopped onion between; cover with crackers that have been soaked soft in milk, pour over it two gills of white wine, and two of water; put on the top of the oven, and stew it gently about an hour; take it out carefully, and lay it in a deep dish; thicken the gravy with a little flour and a spoonful of butter, add some chopped parsley, boil it a few minutes, and pour it over the fish— serve it up hot.

In the South, things were a bit different because their warmer climate afforded them a longer growing season. But here, too, European ways of doing things were replaced by and integrated into new ways of doing things. The Native American peoples of the Southeast introduced Southerners to new varieties of vegetables such as squash, pumpkins, many types of beans, tomatoes (which the early settlers thought were poisonous!), and one of the most important new crops, corn. Southern settlers brought European livestock like cows and pigs, but Native Americans encouraged them to hunt deer and small game animals like squirrels and rabbit. The fertile land of the American South was a new, exciting beginning for many Europeans who had left small plots of land in Europe for hundred-acre tracts in the New World. Of course, not everyone had access to land to grow their own food: the Africans brought over to harvest cash crops like tobacco, sugar, and cotton were forced to create new dishes from whatever whites allowed them to have.

Native Americans had their own ways of preparing and preserving foods.

TO DRESS A TURTLE

Cut off the head and let it bleed well. Separate the bottom shell from the top with care, for fear of breaking the gall bag. Throw the liver and eggs, if any, into a bowl of water. Slice off all the meat from the undershell and put in water also; break the shell in pieces, wash carefully and place it in a pot; cover it with water, and add one pound of middling or flitch of bacon with four chopped onions. Set this on the fire to boil. (If preferred, open and clean the chitterlings or intestines also—some use them.) Let this boil gently for four hours; keep the liver to fry. While the undershell is boiling, wash the top-shell neatly, cut all the meat out, cover it up and set it by. Parboil the fins, clean them perfectly; take off the black skin and throw them into water. Now cut the flesh removed from both shells into small pieces; cut the fins up; sprinkle with salt, cover and set them by. When the pot containing the shells, etc., has boiled four hours, take out the bacon, scrape the shell, clean and strain the liquor, pour back in the pot about one quart, and put the rest by for the soup. Pick out the nice pieces strained out, and put with the fins in the gravy. Add to the meat one bottle of wine, one gill mushroom catsup, one gill of lemon pickle, cloves, nutmeg, salt, pepper, and one pound fresh butter rolled in flour. Stew together; take out the herbs, thicken with flour and put in the shell to bake with a puff paste around it. Trim with eggs.

In 1804, President Jefferson's Louisiana Purchase opened up the western frontier and expanded the United States' territory. At that time, the American West was still largely the domain of Native Americans, hunters, trappers, and frontiersmen. For a long time, settlers in the West relied heavily on the aid of Native Americans to survive (they didn't have a choice!). But slowly, as the nation began to move westward, the township became the center of life in western territories. Settlers cleared small plots of land, sometimes for farming, sometimes just for a log cabin, and they relied heavily on the supplies of the local general store, which had everything from dried meats to new shoes to salt. The general store was often the only thing connecting settlers to civilization.

In general, the earliest western settlers had even less choice over what foods they could eat because so few European-style foods were available. The "American" diet of today, with its emphasis on meat, actually began during this time period,

when settlers were more likely to hunt and trap animals than to grow their food. Animals both small and large were in abundance in early America, and settlers moving west often used meat as a way to stay alive when they couldn't farm or garden.

FRIED SQUIRREL

(a frontier recipe from 1818)

Rinse skinned squirrel in cold water and pat dry. Dip in buttermilk and then in seasoned flour, and fry in hot fat. If the squirrel is young, steaming is not necessary. Otherwise, drain off excess fat and add a cup of water and steam covered. Make gravy in the frying pan by adding leftover seasoned flour and milk or water. Serve with biscuits and wild plum jelly.

RACCOON

The best way to cook a coon is to leave the coon whole after gutting and leave it to soak all night in salt water. Parboil the coon for a little while and then take out of the water and fill the chest cavity with sweet potatoes. Then bake in the oven until brown and tender.

Most Americans in the early 1800s lived on small farms and Thomas Jefferson's ideal for the new nation was a society of small farmers, with little distinction between the rich and the poor. Many Europeans came to the New World looking only for a small piece of land where they might provide for themselves and their family. They were what is called subsistence farmers—farmers who grew only what they needed to survive, and used their surplus (leftover) crops to trade for whatever goods they couldn't make themselves.

Immigrant Influence

The Germans were one of the first and largest waves of immigrant to arrive in the U.S. and they brought with them an emphasis on marinated meats, sour flavors, wursts, pastries, and beer. The German emphasis on meat was especially well adapted to America, where meat was already so popular. Over the years, the German influence on American food would result in such standards as barbeque, hotdogs, donuts, and hamburgers. Later in the century, huge waves of immigrants from Ireland, Poland, and Italy would bring entirely new tastes into the mix.

Different types of sausages were popular in different parts of Europe, but Germans were especially fond of them. Making sausages—using salting, spicing, and smoking—was a way of preparing meat so it could be kept longer without going bad.

EYEWITNESS ACCOUNT

The Frugal Housewife

The following is an excerpt on how to properly store vegetables from an 1830 publication by Lydia Maria Francis Child, called *The Frugal Housewife, Dedicated to Those Who Are Not Ashamed of Economy:*

Parsnips should be kept down cellar covered up in sand, entirely excluded from the air. They are good only in the spring.

Cabbages put into a hole in the ground will keep well during the winter, and be hard, fresh, and sweet, in the spring. Many farmers keep potatoes in the same way.

Onions should be kept very dry; and never carried into the cellar except in severe weather, when there is danger of their freezing. By no means let them be in the cellar after March; they will sprout and spoil. Potatoes should likewise be carefully looked to in the spring, and the sprouts broken off. The cellar is the best place for them, because they are injured by wilting; but sprout them carefully, if you want to keep them. They never sprout but three times; therefore, after you have sprouted them three times, they will trouble you no more.

Squashes should never be kept down cellar when it is possible to prevent it. Dampness injures them. If intense cold makes it necessary to put them there, bring them up as soon as possible, and keep them in some dry, warm place.

Part II
1840–1865 Food for Pioneers, Slaves, and Soldiers

1830

1830 (-39) US Agricultural exports $74 million a year during the 1830s—higher than any previous decade.

1834

1834 Oberlin Stove is invented by Philo Stewart. A compact, wood-burning, cast-iron stove that would sell some 90,000 units in the next 30 years.

1838

1838 Trail of Tears—General Winfield Scott and 7,000 troops force Cherokees to walk from Georgia to a reservation set up for them in Oklahoma (nearly 1,000 miles). Around 4,000 Native Americans die during the journey.

1838 The first state temperance law is passed in Tennessee, banning the sale of alcohol.

1848

1848 Seneca Falls Convention—Feminist convention held for women's suffrage and equal legal rights.

1848(-58) California Gold Rush—Over 300,000 people flock to California in search of gold.

1854

1854 Kansas-Nebraska Act—States that each new state entering the country will decide for themselves whether or not to allow slavery. This goes directly against the terms agreed upon in the Missouri Compromise of 1820.

1860

1860 The Pony Express begins delivering mail across the Great Plains and Rocky Mountains to the West.

PONY EXPRESS

1839

1839 The first camera is patented by Louis Daguerre.

1840

1840 The US population is 17,069,453. Farmers make up 69% of the work force.

1844

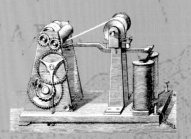

1844 First public telegraph line in the world is opened—between Baltimore and Washington.

of the 1800s

1861

1861(-65) Civil War —Fought between the Union and Confederate states.

1862

1862 Emancipation Proclamation— Lincoln states that all slaves in Union states are to be freed.

1865

1865 Thirteenth Amendment to the United States Constitution— Officially abolishes slavery across the country.

1865 President Abraham Lincoln is assassinated on April 15.

By the middle of the 1800s, most parts of the West were well on their way to being settled. During these years there was a rush for Western lands. Many settlers were looking for gold, but most were simply looking for the cheap and bountiful land they had heard so much about. In 1840, there were only 150 Americans living in Oregon, but by 1860, tens of thousands of settlers had made the long and treacherous trek to Oregon known as the Oregon Trail. So strong was the lure of the West, that men and women were willing to risk their very lives to take one of the longest and most difficult land journeys in history just to claim land that they had never seen before.

Pioneers might be able to bring along one or two cows as they traveled west, but any more than that wasn't practical.

Food was one of the biggest challenges for the wagon trains heading west. First of all, many pioneers were poor farmers or immigrants with little more than the shirts on their backs. These pioneers could either go into debt to a supplier or risk the journey with few supplies. Those who could afford to stock a wagon for the trip had to plan carefully. Fruits and vegetables were nearly impossible to keep fresh on the long trail. Pioneers often suffered from scurvy, a disease resulting from vitamin deficiency. Trail food had to be compact, lightweight, and nonperishable. Most pioneers relied on dried foods, especially dried meats, to nourish themselves. Sometimes they brought cattle along which could provide fresh milk and meat, but animals were difficult to keep alive on the trail, and sometimes an entire herd would be gone by the time they arrived at their destination.

Meals on the westward trail had to be easy to prepare. Some things could be cooked over the campfire, but everything else had to be eaten as it was.

SHOPPING LIST

Here's what supplies for the Oregon Trail cost during the 1800s:

Pork: 11 cents/lb
Bacon: 12–15 cents/lb
Salt beef: 8–9 cents/lb
Fresh beef: 4–5 cents/lb
Flour: 4–5 cents/lb
Hard bread: 9–10 cents/lb
Beans: 10 cents/quart
Rice: 8–10 cents/lb
Coffee: 12–18 cents/lb
Sugar: 7–8 cents/lb
Vinegar: 6 cents/quart

EYEWITNESS ACCOUNT

Randolph B. Marcy's *A Handbook for Overland Expeditions* was considered by many to be the best manual for westward migration. It contained practical advice on everything from route selection and wagon packing to emergency medicine (rattlesnake bites) and dealing with Native Americans.

Supplies for a march should be put up in the most secure, compact, and portable shape. Bacon should be packed in strong sacks of a hundred pounds to each; or, in very hot climates, put in boxes and surrounded with bran, which in a great measure prevents the fat from melting away. If pork be used, in order to avoid transporting about forty per cent. Of useless weight, it should be taken out of the barrels and packed like bacon; then so placed in the bottom of the wagons as to keep it cool. The pork, if well cured, will keep several months in this way, but bacon is preferable.

Flour should be packed in stout double canvas sacks well sewed, a hundred pounds in each sack. Butter may be preserved by boiling it thoroughly, and skimming off the scum as it rises to the top until it is quite clear like oil. It is then placed in tin canisters and soldered up. This mode of preserving butter has been adopted in the hot climate of southern Texas, and it is found to keep sweet for a great length of time, and its flavor is but little impaired by the process. Sugar may be well secured in India-rubber or gutta-percha sacks, or so placed in the wagon as not to risk getting wet.

Desiccated or dried vegetables are almost equal to the fresh, and are put up in such a compact a portable form as easily to be transported over the plains.

As mining towns sprang up, men arrived ready to get rich from gold. Those who gave up on gold and instead opened a restaurant often made out much better, though.

Many settlers started farms or ranches in Iowa, Missouri, Montana, and Idaho. But the biggest draw to the West Coast was, of course, California.

California in the 1800s is most famous for the gold rush of 1849, which brought eighty thousand gold-seekers, called "forty-niners," to that westernmost territory. Over

WHAT'S ON THE MENU?

This was the bill of fare at the What Cheer Restaurant in the 1850s:

Boiled mutton with oyster sauce, 10 cents
Roast beef with lima beans, 10 cents
Pig's feet, soused or in batter, 10 cents
Beefsteak and onions, with fried potatoes, 10 cents
Stewed mutton with bread, butter and potatoes, 5 cents
Buckwheat cakes with honey, 5 cents
Clam chowder, 5 cents
Cup of chocolate (hot chocolate), 5 cents
Chicken potpie, 20 cents
Porterhouse steak, 25 cents
Baked apples, 5 cents
Stewed prunes, 5 cents
Mammoth glass of Mason Celebrated Beer, 5 cents
Roast turkey and currant jelly, 25 cents
Hot oatmeal mush, 10 cents

three-quarters of those seekers were American, and they brought their American tastes and preferences along with them. California itself was an extremely diverse environment with a lot of agricultural potential that got put on hold when the gold-hunters arrived. Before the gold rush, the territory had been settled by small numbers of Mexican and American farmers and ranchers. The gold rush changed everything.

Like much of the frontier culture in the West, California's mining towns were largely composed of men; in fact, in the 1850s it was estimated that women made up only 8 percent of California's total population. And yet more men were pouring into the state every day, almost all of whom spent their energy and efforts in the mines, and not in the kitchen. What resulted was a food culture dependent on small restaurants.

The restaurants that served the early mining towns were of all shapes and sizes, but for a long time they had one thing in common: high prices. Because the agricultural economy had been put on hold for the mining economy, almost everything had to be imported to California, and because the rush of settlers was largely composed of Americans, the established Mexican and Chinese cuisines were ignored or dismissed. Miners wanted familiar foods, and were willing to pay high prices to get them. Men who struck gold were known to pay huge sums for elaborate French cuisine—oysters, puddings, even champagne—brought in by ship and by land. Those that weren't so lucky had to make due with dried jerky and whatever vegetables were available at the dining places. But even vegetables were expensive, and the early miners often remarked with disgust that vegetables out West were sold by the pound, not by the bushel. Eventually, things would level out. People decided to settle more permanently, bringing their families and cultivating the land.

Soldiers and settlers alike ate hardtack in the nineteenth century, mainly because it consisted only of flour, salt, and water, making the bread-like food very inexpensive.

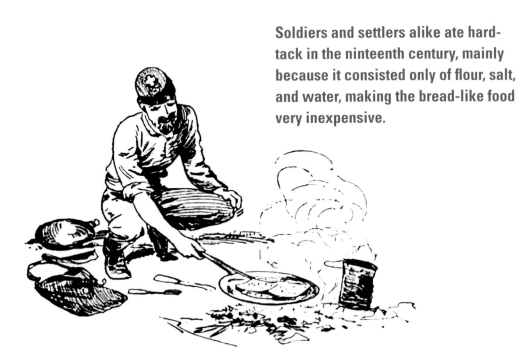

FRYING HARDTACK.

EYEWITNESS ACCOUNT

A forty-niner, writing in his journal, described a meeting with another wagon train:

Their sugar, rice, beans & flour were also out & they had been living on nothing but hardtack & coffee, & coffee & hardtack. They had no shot guns & of course took no game. This reconciled us, I assure you, & we censured ourselves for our past time growling, & find, instead of suffering, we have been feasting on salt pork and jack rabbits.

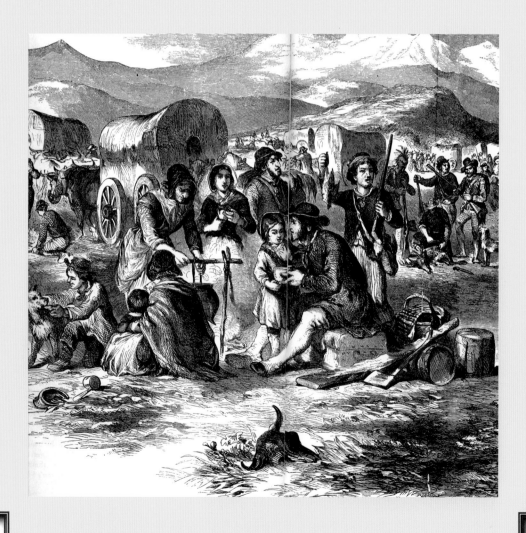

Slavery

By the middle-1800s, many African slaves were second or even third-generation slaves, born in America and born into the slave system. There was no single condition under which all slaves lived—every situation was unique in some way to the owner, to the type of crops being harvested, and to the climate in which they lived. (Of course, the fundamental inequality between master and slave remained the same, regardless of the situation.)

When you think of slavery, you may imagine slaves living on massive plantations in groups of two-hundred or more. While such large plantations certainly did exist, they were not the norm. In fact, the average slave-holding house had less than twenty slaves. Some households allowed their slaves to grow their own vegetable gardens, while others did not. Those that didn't worried that these gardens would take their slaves away from the work of the plantation. Most slaves in the South had diets that were inadequate to the hard, labor-intensive work they performed every day—and their "owners" did this intentionally. Among slave-owners there was constant fear of slave rebel-

The slaves who lived in these cabins were responsible for preparing their own meals, possibly with food they grew themselves.

EYEWITNESS ACCOUNT

In 1909, Annie Burton recorded her memories of growing up in slavery. She wrote:

We children had no supper, and only a little piece of bread or something of the kind in the morning. Our dishes consisted of one wooden bowl, and oyster-shells were our spoons. This bowl served for about fifteen children, and often the dogs and the ducks and the peafowl had a dip in it. Sometimes we had buttermilk and bread in our bowl, sometimes greens or bones.

lion, and a poor diet was one way in which owners could keep slaves weak.

But from the moment they arrived in the New World, slaves began finding creative and inventive ways to feed and nourish themselves. Many Euro-peans observers remarked that slaves ate a much wider variety of native nuts and vegetables than their white own-ers. They used whatever small piece of land they were given to grow whatever grain, vegetables, and fruits they could.

Food and the Civil War

The outbreak of the Civil War in 1861 put a strain on food systems across the country. Civilians as well as soldiers had to change their diets. Boys and men moved off the farm and into the camp. In general, the armies of the North ate better than the armies of the South. But this is only a generalization; the men in both armies had to fend for themselves, and suffered better or worse food as they were able to find it in the field. Every army had a few "sutlers"—men who brought luxury items like tobacco, candy, and fine foods to soldiers in exchange for money. On a larger scale, each army had its own methods of requesting food from the civilians in the countryside where they were stationed. Oftentimes these "requests" were more like demands, especially when they came from armed and starving men!

Food was central to the soldier's life. From sun up to sun down, a soldier was concerned with two things: drill, and food—or, as the case might often be, finding food. Drill practice involved cleaning and loading a musket, forming

A soldier in the Civil War would have been fortunate to get food such as this stew. Often, the rations might only include hardtack and a bit of dried fruit.

ranks, and executing military maneuvers. Food was rationed out uncooked and usually a group of men would combine their rations for a shared meal. Groups such as these were called "messes" and they had the benefit of sharing ingredients for a better meal. The armies of the North had the advantage for most of the war because the factories and industries of the North were better able to supply and ship food.

One of the most common, and disliked, army food supplies was called "hardtack," a nickname the soldiers gave to the hard, cracker-like bread that was regularly shipped in large quantities to their camps. Other very common camp foods were coffee and dried meat. This was hardly a sufficient diet for men constantly outdoors, putting their lives in danger.

HARDTACK BREAD

5 cups flour
1 cup water
1 tbs salt

Mix all ingredients thoroughly. Knead dough and roll out till it is 1/2 inch thick. Cut dough into 3x3 squares, and poke a 3x3 series of holes in the center, evenly spaced. Bake in preheated oven, 425 degrees until dry and lightly golden brown. Be sure to keep dry. If they get damp, they will get moldy quickly and cannot be eaten. If you have any weevils or maggots throw them in for added nutritional value!

Back East

While soldiers, slaves, and frontier families were eating foods that were far from luxurious, people in the more civilized regions of the East consumed foods that had become traditional and routine. The following "Bill of Fare for the Winter" from a cooking manual published in 1853 lays out a suggested meal plan for a middle class family in Philadelphia:

Monday

Breakfast: Corn bread, cold bread, stew, boiled eggs.

Dinner: Soup, cold joint, calves' head, vegetables.

Dessert: Puddings, etc.

Tea: Cold bread, milk toast, stewed fruit.

Tuesday

Breakfast: Hot cakes, cold bread, sausages, fried potatoes.

Dinner: Soup, roast turkey, cranberry sauce, boiled ham, vegetables.

Dessert: Pie, etc.

Tea: Corn bread, cold bread, stewed oysters.

Wednesday

Breakfast: Hot bread, cold bread, chops, omelet.

Dinner: Boiled mutton, stewed liver, vegetables.

Dessert: Pudding, etc.

Tea: Hot light bread, cold bread, fish, stewed fruit.

Thursday

Breakfast: Hot cakes, cold bread, sausages, fried potatoes.

Dinner: Soup, poultry, cutlets, vegetables.

Dessert: Custards and stewed fruit.

Tea: Corn bread, cold bread, frizzled beef, stewed fruits, or soused calves' feet.

Friday

Breakfast: Hot bread, cold bread, chops, omelet.

Dinner: Soup, fish, roast mutton and currant jelly, vegetables.

Dessert: Pudding.

Tea: Hot light bread, cold bread, stewed fruit.

Saturday

Breakfast: Hot bread, a nice hash, fried potatoes.

Dinner: Soup, roast veal, steaks, oyster pie, vegetables.

Dessert: Custards.

Tea: Corn bread, cold bread, stewed oysters.

Sunday

Breakfast: Cold bread, croquets, omelet.

Dinner: Roast pig, apple sauce, steaks, vegetables.

Dessert: Pie, jelly.

Tea: Cold bread, stewed fruit, light cake.

Part III
1866–1900
Industrial Food

1867

1867 United States purchases Alaska from Russia.

1867 The Chicago Lake Tunnel is finished. It is the first water supply tunnel for a U.S. city, bringing thousands of gallons of fresh water to residents.

1869

1869 Transcontinental Railroad completed on May 10.

1869 Frozen food is shipped long distance for first time. Frozen Texas beef is shipped by steamship to New Orleans.

1870

1870 Fifteenth Amendment to the United States Constitution—Prohibits any citizen from being denied to vote based on their "race, color, or previous condition of servitude."

1870 Christmas is declared a national holiday.

1886

1886 The Statue of Liberty is dedicated on October 28.

1890

1890 Wounded Knee Massacre— Last battle in the American Indian Wars.

1892

1892 Ellis Island is opened to receive immigrants coming into New York.

1876

1876 Alexander Graham Bell invents the telephone.

1876 New York Cooking School founded by Juliet Corson.

1877

1877 Great Railroad Strike—Often considered the country's first nationwide labor strike.

1878

1878 Thomas Edison patents the phonograph on February 19.

1878 Thomas Edison invents the light bulb on October 22.

1880

1880 US Population is 50,155,783. Farmers have dropped to 49% of labor force.

of the 1800s

1894

1894 Coca Cola is first bottled in Vicksburg, Mississippi. Prior to this date, it was only mixed to order at the soda fountain.

1896

1896 Plessy vs. Ferguson—Supreme Court case that rules that racial segregation is legal as long as accommodations are kept equal.

1896 Henry Ford builds his first combustion-powered vehicle, which he names the Ford Quadricycle.

1898

1898 The Spanish-American War—The United States gains control of Cuba, Puerto Rico, and the Philippines.

As the 1800s came to a close, and with the Union kept intact by the victory of the industrial North in the Civil War, America began to enter a new, industrial age, following the path that Europe was already taking. Between 1800 and 1900, Europe's population more than doubled—but in that same period, the population of the United States practically exploded! In one hundred years, the U.S. population grew from about 6 million to over 76 million people.

America was expanding at speeds never seen before. Huge masses of immigrants were arriving to fill the growing need for factory workers. Suddenly America, like England before it, had a true industrial economy, and the newly arrived immigrants were just the right candidates for low-wage

factory labor. Several contradictory trends emerged at once: while wealthy factory-owners and "barons" of industry grew ever richer, and the masses of their workers remained in poverty, a new middle-class was growing. As the economy, and the population, grew, the need for lawyers, doctors, teachers, and accountants grew as well.

John D. Rockefeller, one of the wealthiest Americans of the ninteenth century.

Men who worked hard in the steel mills all day had no time left over to grow or hunt food. They depended on the developing food industry to do that part for them.

The intercontinental railroad allowed different kinds of food to be sent all over the country.

More people than ever before were living in cities. In many cases, conditions for poor immigrants were no better, or even worse, than the conditions they left behind in their native lands. Lacking any land of their own, the poor depended on low wages to buy food from the surrounding countryside. Mechanical milkers and glass bottling, as well as refrigeration, made it possible for farmers to ship fresh, cold milk to the city. The old system of people growing their own food was disappearing, and being replaced by an exchange of goods and services between rural and urban areas.

A number of inventions made these changes in food systems possible. Two of these were the steam engine and the locomotive (or train). Together, these made for a powerful machine that could move men and products far distances, and quickly. In addition, the Civil War had brought the invention of the "refrigerated rail car," and now it was first put to use in Illinois.

The drugstore of Caleb Bradham, inventor of Pepsi, as portrayed at the Historical Museum in New Bern, North Carolina. Like many pharmacists at the turn of the century, Bradham had a soda fountain in his drugstore, where he served his customers refreshing drinks he created himself. His most popular beverage was made of carbonated water, sugar, vanilla, rare oils, pepsin, and cola nuts; he eventually named it "Pep Cola." By the end of the 19th century, Americans no longer drank as much cider. Hard cider was alcoholic, and the temperance movement inspired some farmers to even cut down their apple trees, so they wouldn't be tempted to imbibe. "Soft drinks" like Pepsi Cola began to replace the "hard drinks," such as cider and beer. A new era of food and drink was coming to America.

A refrigerated rail car was just what it sounds like: a railroad car kept cold enough to transport goods like milk, raw meats, and other perishables. Illinois was the natural place for the refrigerated rail car to be born because it was already the middleman between East and West. Ranchers in the West would drive their teams of cattle hundreds of miles to be slaughtered and shipped back East. During the long journey their cattle lost weight and many died before they reached the railways. The refrigerated rail car, however, allowed livestock to be slaughtered and shipped long distances. Rather than try to keep cattle alive on long train-rides East, they could be slaughtered in the West and their meat kept fresh. This opened up a much bigger market for ranchers and meat-packers.

Food producers of all sorts began to realize the possibilities opened to them by the industrial age. Food became a product, capable of being standardized.

An ambitious food businessman could produce his food item in large quantities, can or bottle it, and ship it anywhere in the world. For the most part, the rich and the urban were the first consumers of these new industrial foods. Food in most American homes was still the result of local farming.

Between 1866 and 1886, around 20 million cattle were herded across country from Texas to Kansas, which was the closest access to the railroad. Towns and cities grew up along the route to provide for the needs of the cowboys.

But the way that food was cooked had begun to change. The middle and upper classes who could afford to update their kitchens now had a range of appliances to choose from: state-of-the-art ovens that allowed cooks to control temperatures, pastry cutters, jelly moulds, biscuit tins, graters, peelers, mincers, and slicers. Gadgets of all shapes and sizes entered the kitchen to make old chores easier and more effi-

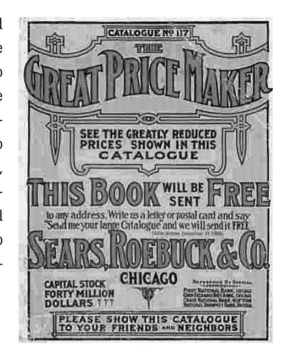

White Mountain Freezer
(TRIPLE MOTION)

The "World's Best" Ice-Cream Freezer

This World-Famous Freezer

Makes the most perfect ice-creams and sherbets in a very few minutes, as well as an unlimited variety of delicious frozen fruits, puddings, and chilled dainties at a very trifling cost. It will surprise you to learn the great extent of "White Mountain" usefulness. Send for our recipe book, "Frozen Dainties," which tells everything you need to know about the making of the most delicious desserts and gives about one hundred recipes.

THE WHITE MOUNTAIN FREEZER COMPANY
NASHUA, N. H.

cient. Cast iron and tin-plated equipment took the place of old brass and copper. Now the middle class person could prepare the complicated and difficult dishes that were once reserved for the upper classes only.

People from all over the country could purchase such fine kitchen equipment. It didn't matter where you lived—in rural Minnesota or urban San Francisco, Americans found ways to get their products to consumers. One famous example of the shipping system was Sears, Roebuck, & Co, a business that began as a mail-order catalogue in

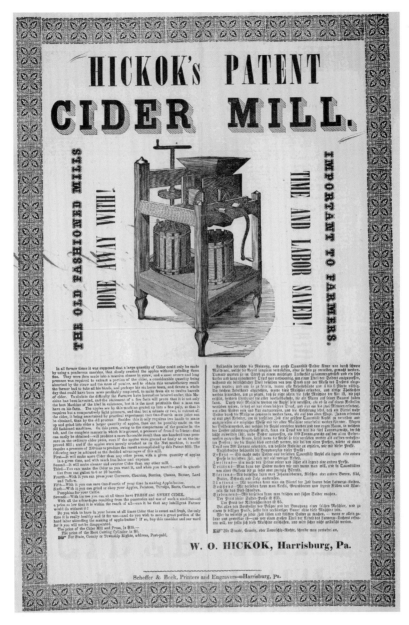

the 1890s. Richard Sears established the system when he saw farmers coming into town to sell food and purchase goods. The catalogue allowed people to look over a list of prices for foods and other products. By 1900, a person with a Sears-Roebuck catalogue could purchase anything from a frozen bag of vegetables to an ice cream maker, cider press—or even an automobile or a house!

Health Concerns

Advances in crafting lenses led to the improvement of the first microscope in the late 1800s, which in turn led to the discovery of bacteria and germs in general. This had a huge impact on the lives of ordinary people. As scientists and doctors began to study these extremely tiny enemies, they began for the first time to understand the reasons for so many illnesses. People had known for a long time, out of practical experience and knowledge, that old or rotten food could cause illness, but these new discoveries showed that even food that looked fresh or clean could contain disease-causing germs.

In many cities, conditions near the end of the 1800s were extremely unsanitary. Public sewage systems were still being developed, and fresh water was always hard to find. Many reform movements began at this time in an effort to combat the increasingly filthy and impoverished conditions of America's major cities. Journalists like Jacob Riis published works (his most famous was called *How the Other Half Lives*) in which they documented with photographs the hunger, poverty, and tight living quarters of the urban poor.

This image, taken by Jacob Riis for his book *How the Other Half Lives*, shows street children sleeping in a corner. These children found food however they could, usually by begging, stealing, or finding scraps in the garbage.

EYEWITNESS ACCOUNT

The following is a passage from Upton Sinclair's novel *The Jungle*, a book that revealed the horrors of the meat-packing industry in late-1800s Chicago:

The meat would be shoveled into carts, and the man who did the shoveling would not trouble to lift out a rat even when he saw one—there were things that went into the sausage in comparison with which a poisoned rat was a tidbit. There was no place for the men to wash their hands before they ate their dinner, and so they made a practice of washing them in the water that was to be ladled into the sausage.

The Spirit of Innovation

It was a new age for food. A spirit of innovation was alive throughout the land. Like never before, people were experimenting with new ways of cooking, combining, and selling food. This was the era of Cream of Wheat, Shredded Wheat, Coca-Cola, Juicy Fruit gum, and Cracker Jack. The idea of developing and branding new food products was not itself a new idea, but doing it on such a large scale, and selling it to a national and international market was.

The Chicago World's Fair in 1893 was one of the best expressions of America's thriving sense of creativity and wonder. The fair was truly a world event, with guests from Hawaii, China, and Russia. Americans came to the event by the thousands, hoping to get a look at Hawaiian hula dancers, get a seat on the world's first Ferris wheel, and sample foods from around the country. In addition, much of the fair was powered by electricity—a fairly new invention at the time—and had phosphorescent and neon lights.

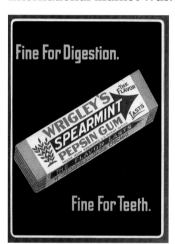

Americans crowded through the exhibit halls to see the newest inventions that would one day change their lives. Most went home from the fair to houses lit by candles and milked their cows by hand, just as they had always done. But the seeds of a technological revolution were planted. The future was on its way. And people would always need to eat!

Think About It

The average American in the 1800s ate a diet made up of locally produced food and drink. Supplies were sometimes limited and some modern food cleanliness standards were just becoming standardized.

From what you've learned in this book, compare what an average American young person in 1850 ate on a typical day to what you eat in your typical day.

- What are the differences in your diet compared to theirs?

- Are there foods in the daily diet of a young person in 1850 that are not in yours (or in yours that were not in theirs)? Give some examples.

- What do you both eat that hasn't changed much since the 1800s?

- Which diet do you think is better for a person's health?

Words Used in This Book

branding: Giving a product a name by which it is identified and marketed.

consumers: The people who buy and use a product.

contradictory: Things that are, or seem to be, in disagreement.

diverse: An environment with a wide variety of climates, landscapes, and agricultural potential.

frontier: An area that is newly settled and where conditions are often rough.

meat-packers: People involved in the business of slaughtering, butchering, and processing meat for sale.

nonperishable: Food items that can be stored for long periods without rotting or becoming stale.

reform: To improve something by correcting errors or abuses.

sensual: Having to do with the enjoyment of physical pleasure.

standardized: Things that are produced from the same set of ingredients and at a certain measurable standard of quality.

wursts: The German word for sausages, of which there are many, many kinds.

Find Out More

In Books

Davis, William C. *A Taste for War: The Culinary History of the Blue and the Gray.* Mechanicsburg, Penn.: Stackpole Books, 2003.

Eisnach, Dwight, Herbert C. Covey. *What the Slaves Ate: Recollections of African American Foods and Foodways from the Slave Narratives.* Santa Barbara, Calif.: ABC-CLIO, 2009.

Williams, Susan. *Food in the United States, 1820s-1890.* Santa Barbara, Calif.: Greenwood Press, 2006.

On the Internet

Food of Nineteenth-Century United States
library.thinkquest.org/C005446/Food/English/19thcenturyus.html

The History of Canned Food
www.tinplategroup.com/pooled/articles/BF_DOCART/view.asp?Q=BF_DOCART_197927

Texas Pioneer Recipes
www.fortunecity.com/millennium/balloons/1035/1800recp.htm

Victorian Cooking and Kitchens
19thcentury.wordpress.com/2007/11/21/victorian-cooking-kitchens-1

Index

Picture Credits

About the Author and the Consultant

Zachary Chastain is an independent writer and actor living in Binghamton, New York. He is the author of various educational books for both younger and older audiences.

John Gillis is a Rutgers University Professor of History Emeritus. A graduate of Amherst College and Stanford University, he has taught at Stanford, Princeton, University of California at Berkeley, as well as Rutgers. Gillis is well known for his work in social history, including pioneering studies of age relations, marriage, and family. The author or editor of ten books, he has also been a fellow at both St. Antony's College, Oxford, and Clare Hall, Cambridge.